This book belongs to

_____

This book is dedicated to my children - Mikey, Kobe, and Jojo.
Adaptability = your key to success.

978-1-953399-81-6 Printed and bound in the USA. GrowGrit.co

eNinja

By Mary Nhin

Pictures by
Jelena Stupar

Sure, I will! The thing about online school is that it's just like going to real school except we don't leave the house.

I'll let you in on a little secret I use to succeed at online school. It's called the:

I am Prepared.

By charging my device the night before, I'll be much happier and not have to worry about missing out on online school.

Since I don't have a separate room, I sit in my favorite chair at the dining room table. That's where it's quiet in my house and I have a lot of natural light.

I have all of my classroom supplies ready for use and near me.

I like being ready. That means I get dressed, use the restroom, and eat a hearty meal before class.

It may be easy to stay in my pajamas but I'll be more ready to tackle obstacles if I get dressed as if I were leaving the house.

Doing these things help put me in the right mindset.

I'm always about 10 minutes early to class so that I can test my internet connection, mute my mic, and turn on my camera. I make sure to have my screen on gallery view so I can see all of my friends and teacher.

By being punctual, I show respect for my teacher's and classmates' time.

Testing, testing 1, 2, 3...

I am Polite.

I don't know about you but having my tablet and devices out tempt me to pick them up and play with them so I hide them.

Online etiquette

 Ears are listening.

 Eyes are looking.

 Mouth is quiet.

Hands are still.

 Body is facing the screen.

 Brain is thinking.

I turn off or eliminate any background noise, and I sit in a designated work space during online class.

When I have a question, I raise my hand and wait until I'm called on. Or I follow my teacher's guidelines on how to ask questions. Some teachers like it when their students use the questions or chat box while others prefer email.

I ask early and I'm not afraid to ask questions, but only when it's my turn.

I am Positive

No matter what happens, I try to stay positive. If things go wrong, which they do a lot, I remind myself that I'm trying my best.

Things may change often but if we remain flexible and positive, everything will turn out okay.

Positivity is key.

I like keeping a schedule and using checklists to mark items off as I complete them. This helps me to feel like I've achieved something.

Remembering the 3 P's could be your secret weapon against online school disaster.

Download the free eNinja Cheat Sheet for online school success at
marynhin.com/ninja-printables.html

@marynhin @GrowGrit
#NinjaLifeHacks

Mary Nhin Grow Grit

Grow Grit

Advanced learning tips:

1. Remember the 20-20-20 rule created by eye doctors for your eye health:

Every 20 minutes, look up for 20 seconds at something 20 feet away. If you know you'll be online for a long time, remember the 20-20-20.

2. Make time for friends, even if it means seeing them virtually.

3. Exercising daily will keep you very positive.

4. Revisit your schedule. How did it work for you? Do you need to revise your plan?

5. Self reflect on the experience learning from a distance. Look in the mirror; smile; say you are proud of yourself and pat yourself on the back!

6. Share your learning with someone at home!

Virtual Meeting Success Cheat Sheet

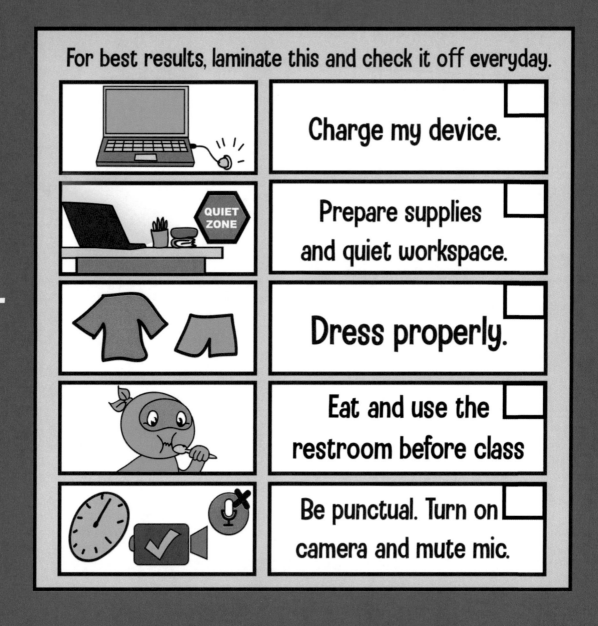

Be Prepared

For best results, laminate this and check it off everyday.

Charge my device.

Prepare supplies and quiet workspace.

Dress properly.

Eat and use the restroom before class

Be punctual. Turn on camera and mute mic.

Be Polite

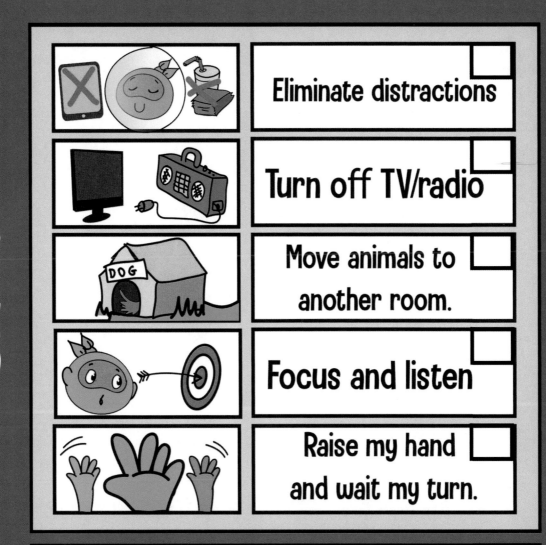

Eliminate distractions	☐
Turn off TV/radio	☐
Move animals to another room.	☐
Focus and listen	☐
Raise my hand and wait my turn.	☐

Be Positive

Say positive things to myself.	☐
Use checklists and schedules to feel accomplished.	☐